US Citizenship Test Study Guide 2026-2027

US Naturalization Prep Book for all 128 USCIS Questions and Answers [8th Edition]

J. M. Lefort

Copyright © 2025 J. M. Lefort

All rights reserved.

ISBN 13: 9781637754269

Table of Contents

Introduction 1

American Government 5

Principles of American Government 5

System of Government 12

Rights and Responsibilities 33

American History 40

Colonial Period and Independence 40

1800s 49

Recent American History and Other
Important Historical Information 54

Symbols and Holidays 65

Symbols 65

Holidays 67

Test Yourself 70

Introduction

Function of the Test

The naturalization test is for non-U.S. citizens who are hoping to become U.S. citizens. The naturalization test is given during the U.S. citizenship interview. After the U.S. citizenship interview is passed, you will take an Oath of Allegiance at a naturalization ceremony.

Test Administration and Format

Those who wish to become U.S. citizens must first apply for naturalization and make sure they meet the requirements. Then the naturalization test will be given at the naturalization interview.

During the naturalization interview, a USCIS officer will ask questions about your background and application. You will then take an English test and a civics test. This guide is only for the civics test. We have provided the 128 possible test questions. You will be asked 20 of these 128 questions during the test. You will have to answer 12 out of 20 questions correctly to pass it.

The civics exam tests you on U.S. history and government knowledge. The questions will be asked to you by a USCIS officer. Then, you will say the answers out loud.

Anyone who fails the naturalization exam will be given a second opportunity to pass. After a second failed attempt, you may reapply for naturalization, or you may appeal the decision.

Note ✽

If you are 65 years old or older and have been a legal permanent resident of the United States for 20 or more years, you may study just the questions that have been marked with an asterisk. You will only be asked 10 questions from that set of 20 questions, and you must answer at least 6 correctly to pass the exam.

Exam Tips

Sometimes a question has multiple correct answers. For example:

3. Name one thing the U.S. Constitution does.

- Forms the government
- Defines powers of government
- Defines the parts of government
- Protects the rights of the people

For this question, all four answers listed are correct. You must only say one of those answers.

Other questions also have multiple correct answers and require you to give multiple answers:

10. Name <u>two</u> important ideas from the Declaration of Independence and the U.S. Constitution.

- Equality
- Liberty
- Social contract
- Natural rights
- Limited government
- Self-government

In this case, all six answers are correct, but you must say two of the answers.

Be sure to read the questions carefully to know how many answers you need to memorize.

Online Resources

Throughout the book are links to our website. Some answers change or are specific to each test taker. The website offers up-to-date information to help you prepare.

You can use this link or scan the QR code with your phone:

apexprep.com/civics

American Government

Principles of American Government

1. What is the form of government of the United States?

- Republic
- Constitution-based federal republic
- Representative democracy

The U.S. government is made up of representatives elected by citizens. These representatives hold official positions in either the central (federal) government or state governments, which hold separate powers. The Constitution guarantees certain rights and defines the government's power.

2. What is the supreme law of the land?*

- (U.S.) Constitution

The highest law is the Constitution. The government cannot pass a law that goes against the Constitution. The Supreme Court can say that state or federal laws are unlawful if a new law goes against the constitution.

3. Name <u>one</u> thing the U.S. Constitution does.

- Forms the government
- Defines powers of government
- Defines the parts of government
- Protects the rights of the people

The Constitution sets up a national government made of three branches: legislative, executive, and judicial. The Constitution also divides federal and state power. Finally, the constitution protects the freedoms of citizens outlined in the Bill of Rights.

4. The U.S. Constitution starts with the words "We the People." What does "We the People" mean?

- Self-government
- Popular sovereignty
- Consent of the governed
- People should govern themselves
- (Example of) social contract

The first sentence of the Constitution (called the Preamble) explains why the Constitution was written. By beginning with "We the People," it invokes a unified collective of all American people. The Constitution defines a government that gets its power from its people, with their consent, and works for the good of its people as part of its binding social contract.

5. How are changes made to the U.S. Constitution?

- Amendments
- The amendment process

Amendments are the only way to change the Constitution. To become a usable part of the Constitution, an amendment must be approved by three-fourths of the legislatures or state ratifying conventions. After the Archivist's consent, the amendment can move forward as part of the Constitution.

6. What does the Bill of Rights protect?

- (The basic) rights of Americans
- (The basic) rights of people living in the United States

The Bill of Rights was approved in 1791. It pledges personal rights and freedoms. It limits government power. It also explains that powers not delegated to Congress should be reserved for the states or the people.

7. How many amendments does the U.S. Constitution have? *

- Twenty-seven (27)

The Constitution has 27 amendments. The first ten amendments were adopted at the same time. These are called the Bill of Rights. It is not ideal for the Constitution to constantly change. This is why amendments must be proposed and approved before going into effect.

8. Why is the Declaration of Independence important?

- It says America is free from British control.
- It says all people are created equal.
- It identifies inherent rights.
- It identifies individual freedoms.

The Declaration of Independence declares that the United States of America is no longer under the authority of Great Britain and is its own sovereign entity. It gives many reasons for this, based on the idea that all people are created equal and have rights and individual freedoms simply by existing.

9. What founding document said the American colonies were free from Britain?

- Declaration of Independence

The Declaration of Independence is a written statement. It announced independence from Great Britain. It declared that the colonies were thirteen independent states. The Declaration of Independence was approved on July 4, 1776.

10. Name <u>two</u> important ideas from the Declaration of Independence and the U.S. Constitution.

- Equality
- Liberty
- Social contract
- Natural rights
- Limited government
- Self-government

Equality denotes that all individuals are equal, regardless of their wealth, power, or status, while Liberty describes guaranteed natural rights and freedoms that all people possess. These founding documents also reflect the ideas that people may enter into a social contract together to create a government for themselves of representatives elected by the people, and that government's power is limited to only the power it is clearly given.

11. The words "Life, Liberty, and the pursuit of Happiness" are in what founding document?

- Declaration of Independence

There are three unalienable Rights mentioned in the Declaration of Independence. These are life, liberty, and the pursuit of happiness. The phrase is taken from this sentence: "We hold these truths to be self-evident, that all men are created equal, that they are endowed by their Creator with certain unalienable Rights, that among these are Life, Liberty and the pursuit of Happiness."

12. What is the economic system of the United States?*

- Capitalism
- Free market economy

The economic system in the United States is a market economy. This means that the U.S. has individual producers and consumers who decide on goods and services. They also decide their own prices. Government plays a limited role in the U.S. market economy. However, it does provide assistance programs, national defense, and interstate highways and airports.

13. What is the rule of law?

- Everyone must follow the law.
- Leaders must obey the law.
- Government must obey the law.
- No one is above the law.

"Rule of law" is how a country's laws influence the society and its people. The rule of law is an ideal where everyone is treated equally before the law. Someone's rank or wealth does not come into consideration under the rule of law. Everyone is treated the same.

14. Many documents influenced the U.S. Constitution. Name <u>one</u>.

- Declaration of Independence
- Articles of Confederation
- Federalist Papers
- Anti-Federalist Papers
- Virginia Declaration of Rights
- Fundamental Orders of Connecticut
- Mayflower Compact
- Iroquois Great Law of Peace

The Founders drew on many sources when writing the Constitution. Some documents were recent (such as the Declaration of Independence and the Articles of Confederation), while others were long-established at the time (such as the Mayflower Compact and the Iroquois Great Law of Peace). All of the documents related to proper governance and rights.

15. There are three branches of government. Why?

- So one part does not become too powerful
- Checks and balances
- Separation of powers

Separation of powers is when the government is divided into separate branches. It keeps one branch from becoming too powerful. In the U.S., the judicial, legislative, and executive branches are separated. They have the power to "check" each other to make sure the balance is equal. The power of these branches to check one another is called "checks and balances."

System of Government

16. Name the three branches of government.

- Legislative, executive, and judicial
- Congress, president, and the courts

The three branches of government are legislative, executive, and judicial. The president is part of the executive branch. Congress makes up the legislative branch. The courts (Supreme Court and lower courts) make up the judicial branch.

17. The President of the United States is in charge of which branch of government?

- Executive branch

The president is head of the executive branch. The executive branch is set up to enforce and execute the law. The president also acts as Commander-in-Chief of the military.

18. What part of the federal government writes laws?

- (U.S.) Congress
- (U.S. or national) legislature
- Legislative branch

The branch that writes the laws is known as the legislative branch. This branch is made up of two chambers: the Senate and the House of Representatives, also known as Congress. The U.S. legislature, Congress, or Senate and House of Representatives are all appropriate answers.

19. What are the <u>two</u> parts of the U.S. Congress?

- Senate and House (of Representatives)

The Senate and House of Representatives make up Congress. This part of the government is considered the bicameral legislative branch. It creates and writes the laws.

20. Name <u>one</u> power of the U.S. Congress.*

- Writes laws
- Declares war
- Makes the federal budget

The U.S. Congress writes and votes on new laws, and can amend those laws later. It is also the only body in the U.S. government that can declare war. Congress also creates federal budget resolutions, which govern spending and taxation.

21. How many U.S. senators are there?

- One hundred (100)

There are 2 Senators chosen to represent each state. There are 50 states. Thus, there are 100 Senators.

22. How long is a term for a U.S. senator?

- Six (6) years

U.S. Senators remain in office for 6 years. One-third of the Senate membership is elected every two years.

23. Who is <u>one</u> of your state's U.S. senators now?

Answers will vary according to your state. You can find your U.S. Senators here:

apexprep.com/civics

Those who live in the District of Columbia or U.S. territories should answer that these places have zero U.S. Senators.

24. How many voting members are in the House of Representatives?

- Four hundred thirty-five (435)

The House of Representatives is part of the U.S. Congress. It is considered the lower chamber. The Senate is considered the upper chamber. The members of the House are elected to states based on population. This is why each number of House members per state is different.

25. How long is a term for a member of the House of Representatives?

- Two (2) years

The House of Representatives is part of the U.S. Congress. It is considered the lower chamber. The Senate is considered the upper chamber. The members of the House are elected to states based on population. This is why each number of House members per state is different.

26. Why do U.S. representatives serve shorter terms than U.S. senators?

- To more closely follow public opinion

The short terms of U.S. Representatives are meant to make them more reactive to the changing needs of their constituents, focused on what the people they represent currently believe is most important for the government to address.

27. How many senators does each state have?

- Two (2)

Two U.S. Senators are elected to represent each state, making a total of 100 U.S. Senators.

28. Why does each state have two senators?

- Equal representation (for small states)
- The Great Compromise (Connecticut Compromise)

When the design for the U.S. government was being worked on, smaller states were worried that states with more people would be too powerful. The Great Compromise in 1787 ensured that the Senate would have equal representation for each state while the number of representatives in the House would be based on population.

29. Name your U.S. representative.

Answers will vary. You can find your U.S. Representative here:

apexprep.com/civics

Some territories may have nonvoting Delegates or Resident Commissioners, or an appropriate answer may be that your territory has no voting Representatives in Congress.

30. What is the name of the Speaker of the House of Representatives now?*

The Speaker of the House of Representatives is the political and parliamentary leader of the House of

Representatives. The Speaker serves as second in line to be president (after the Vice President).

31. Who does a U.S. senator represent?

- Citizens of their state
- People of their state

A U.S. Senator represents the people of their state.

32. Who elects U.S. senators?

- Citizens from their state

U.S. Senators are chosen in statewide elections in the state that they represent. Only voters in that state can vote in that Senate race.

33. Who does a member of the House of Representatives represent?

- Citizens in their (congressional) district
- Citizens in their district
- People from their (congressional) district
- People in their district

Congressional districts are smaller regions within states. There are 435 of these districts across the entire United States of America. Each member of the House of Representatives represents citizens in one district.

34. Who elects members of the House of Representatives?

- Citizens from their (congressional) district

Only voters from a congressional district vote for the representative for their district.

35. Some states have more representatives than other states. Why?

- (Because of) the state's population
- (Because) they have more people
- (Because) some states have more people

The number of U.S. Representatives a state has depends on the state's population. For example, the population of California is 39 million and it has 53 representatives. Likewise, Alaska has a population of 740,000 and has 1 representative.

36. The President of the United States is elected for how many years?*

- Four (4) years

Presidents have four-year terms. After the four years is up, they are able to be elected for another four years. This makes a total of eight years one person can be president. If a president is elected to office through succession (filling a previous president's incomplete term), the greatest number of years they can serve is 10 years, but no more than that.

37. The President of the United States can serve only two terms. Why?

- (Because of) the 22nd Amendment
- To keep the president from becoming too powerful

The 22nd Amendment, ratified in 1951, enacted term limits to prevent any President from accumulating too much personal power by remaining in office for more than two terms.

38. What is the name of the President of the United States now?*

- Donald J. Trump
- Donald Trump
- Trump

Since this can change, visit **apexprep.com/civics** for the latest information.

39. What is the name of the Vice President of the United States now?*

- JD Vance
- Vance

Since this can change, visit **apexprep.com/civics** for the latest information.

40. If the president can no longer serve, who becomes president?

- The Vice President (of the United States)

The Vice President is the first in line to succeed the President were something to happen.

41. Name <u>one</u> power of the president.

- Signs bills into law
- Vetoes bills
- Enforces laws
- Commander in Chief (of the military)
- Chief diplomat
- Appoints federal judges

As head of the Executive branch, the president has been granted specific powers such as signing or vetoing bills from Congress, enforcing laws from ratified bills, setting the goals for international diplomacy, setting strategic goals and means for military operations, and selecting federal judges (who must be confirmed by the U.S. Senate).

42. Who is Commander in Chief of the U.S. military?

- The President (of the United States)

The President is head of the executive office and Commander-in-Chief of the armed forces. This is stated in Article II, Section 2, Clause I of the Constitution.

43. Who signs bills to become laws?

- The President (of the United States)

The bill must pass the Senate and House of Representatives by a majority vote. Then it is sent to the President to sign or veto.

44. Who vetoes bills?*

- The President (of the United States)

The President has the ability to veto bills. If the President vetoes a bill, it goes back to Congress. Congress can then move to revote on the issue.

45. Who appoints federal judges?

- The President (of the United States)

The President appoints nominees for federal judgeships, including vacant seats in the Supreme Court. These nominees must then be confirmed by the U.S. Senate.

46. The executive branch has many parts. Name one.

- President (of the United States)
- Cabinet
- Federal departments and agencies

The President is head of the executive branch, advised by members of the Cabinet. Cabinet secretaries control Executive Departments (such as the Departments of State, Treasury, or Justice), and the executive branch also includes other federal agencies.

47. What does the President's Cabinet do?

- Advises the President (of the United States)

The President appoints the Cabinet with approval from the Senate to be secretaries for the following departments: State, Defense, Labor, Education, Interior, Agriculture, Transportation, Treasury, Energy, Housing and Urban Development, Commerce, Homeland

Security, Health and Human Services, and Veterans Affairs. An additional appointed Cabinet position is the attorney general.

48. What are <u>two</u> Cabinet-level positions?

- Attorney General
- Secretary of Agriculture
- Secretary of Commerce
- Secretary of Education
- Secretary of Energy
- Secretary of Health and Human Services
- Secretary of Homeland Security
- Secretary of Housing and Urban Development
- Secretary of the Interior
- Secretary of Labor
- Secretary of State
- Secretary of Transportation
- Secretary of the Treasury
- Secretary of Veterans Affairs
- Secretary of War
- Vice President
- Administrator of the Environmental Protection Agency
- Administrator of the Small Business Administration
- Director of the Central Intelligence Agency
- Director of the Office of Management and Budget

- Director of National Intelligence
- United States Trade Representative

Appointment members of the Cabinet advise the President and lead executive departments.

49. Why is the Electoral College important?

- It decides who is elected president.
- It provides a compromise between the popular election of the president and congressional selection.

The Electoral College gives each state a number of electoral votes for the Presidency based on its number of Senators and U.S. Representatives. This means that the Electoral College is as balanced in the same way as the U.S. Congress.

50. What is <u>one</u> part of the judicial branch?

- Supreme Court
- Federal Courts

The judicial branch incorporates federal courts, which include the Supreme Court, U.S. District Courts, and the U.S. Court of Appeals.

51. What does the judicial branch do?

- Reviews laws
- Explains laws
- Resolves disputes (disagreements) about the law
- Decides if a law goes against the (U.S.) Constitution

The judicial branch interprets the laws and resolves disputes through the court system. The Supreme Court is the highest court. There are five types of courts that are subordinate to the Supreme Court: United States bankruptcy courts, United States Court of Appeals for the Federal Circuit, United States courts of appeals, United States Court of International Trade, and the United States district courts.

52. What is the highest court in the United States?*

- Supreme Court

The Supreme Court was established in 1789. It has authority over all the other courts in the U.S. One power of the Court is judicial review. Judicial review is the ability to invalidate a law for violating the Constitution. On average, the Supreme Court receives 7,000 cases a year. It agrees to hear only around 150 of those cases.

53. How many seats are on the Supreme Court?

- Nine (9)

There are currently nine seats on the U.S. Supreme Court. While the Supreme Court originally had six members when it was founded, the number of seats fluctuated until 1869 when the current nine seats became permanent.

54. How many Supreme Court justices are usually needed to decide a case?

- Five (5)

Since there are nine justices, five represents a majority when it is time to decide a case. Since nine is an odd number, there is not often a tie vote.

55. How long do Supreme Court justices serve?

- (For) life
- Lifetime appointment
- (Until) retirement

Supreme Court judges serve life terms. Therefore, they serve until they die, retire, or are impeached and removed from the court.

56. Supreme Court justices serve for life. Why?

- To be independent (of politics)
- To limit outside (political) influence

By serving in lifetime terms, Supreme Court justices do not need to worry about reappointment or reelection, which is meant to insulate them from political influence so that they can focus on a free, independent judiciary.

57. Who is the Chief Justice of the United States now?

- John Roberts
- John G. Roberts, Jr.
- Roberts

Since this can change, visit **apexprep.com/civics** for the latest information.

The Chief Justice of the Supreme Court is John Roberts, who has served since 2005.

58. Name one power that is only for the federal government.

- Print paper money
- Mint coins
- Declare war
- Create an army
- Make treaties
- Set foreign policy

The powers given to the federal government are specifically listed in the Constitution under Article I, Section 8. This grants the federal government the power to coin money, regulate commerce, declare war, raise and maintain armed forces, and to establish a Post Office.

59. Name one power that is only for the states.

- Provide schooling and education
- Provide protection (police)
- Provide safety (fire departments)
- Give a driver's license
- Approve zoning and land use

Libraries, schools, police departments, driver's license and parking tickets fall under the state and local governments. The Constitution's tenth amendment explains that "powers not delegated to the United

States by the Constitution ... are reserved to the States respectively, or to the people."

60. What is the purpose of the 10th Amendment?

- (It states that the) powers not given to the federal government belong to the states or to the people.

As part of the concept of a limited government, the 10th Amendment helps ensure that the federal government does not overreach its explicit authority.

61. Who is the governor of your state now?*

Answers will vary.

You can find your Governor here:

apexprep.com/civics

(Note that District of Columbia residents will say that D.C. does not have a Governor).

Governors are the highest-ranking elected officials in the state. Their duties include signing bills into law, serving as commander-in-chief to the state's National Guard, and appointing people to various offices, among others.

62. What is the capital of your state?

Answers will vary. See the table below.

You can find your state's capital here or go to:

apexprep.com/civics

State	Capital
Alabama	Montgomery
Alaska	Juneau
American Samoa	Pago Pago
Arizona	Phoenix
Arkansas	Little Rock
California	Sacramento
Colorado	Denver
Connecticut	Hartford
D.C.	Answer that D.C. is not a state and does not have a capital.
Delaware	Dover
Florida	Tallahassee
Georgia	Atlanta
Guam	Hagåtña
Hawaii	Honolulu
Idaho	Boise
Illinois	Springfield
Indiana	Indianapolis
Iowa	Des Moines

State	Capital
Kansas	Topeka
Kentucky	Frankfort
Louisiana	Baton Rouge
Maine	Augusta
Maryland	Annapolis
Massachusetts	Boston
Michigan	Lansing
Minnesota	Saint Paul
Mississippi	Jackson
Missouri	Jefferson City
Montana	Helena
Nebraska	Lincoln
Nevada	Carson City
New Hampshire	Concord
New Jersey	Trenton
New Mexico	Santa Fe
New York	Albany
North Carolina	Raleigh
North Dakota	Bismarck
Northern Mariana Islands	Saipan
Ohio	Columbus
Oklahoma	Oklahoma City
Oregon	Salem
Pennsylvania	Harrisburg
Puerto Rico	San Juan
Rhode Island	Providence
South Carolina	Columbia

State	Capital
South Dakota	Pierre
Tennessee	Nashville
Texas	Austin
U.S. Virgin Islands	Charlotte Amalie
Utah	Salt Lake City
Vermont	Montpelier
Virginia	Richmond
Washington	Olympia
West Virginia	Charleston
Wisconsin	Madison
Wyoming	Cheyenne

Rights and Responsibilities

63. There are four amendments to the U.S. Constitution about who can vote. Describe <u>one</u> of them.

- Citizens eighteen (18) and older (can vote).
- You don't have to pay (a poll tax) to vote.
- Any citizen can vote. (Women and men can vote.)
- A male citizen of any race (can vote).

The 15th amendment says that all American men of all races can vote. The 19th amendment gave women the right to vote. The 24th amendment made poll taxes illegal. The 26th amendment lowered the voting age from 21 to 18.

64. Who can vote in federal elections, run for federal office, and serve on a jury in the United States?

- Citizens
- Citizens of the United States
- U.S. citizens

Several rights are reserved for citizens of the United States, including voting in federal elections or serving in a federal office. Citizens also have responsibilities such as serving on juries when called.

65. What are **three** rights of everyone living in the United States?

- Freedom of expression
- Freedom of speech
- Freedom of assembly
- Freedom to petition the government
- Freedom of religion
- The right to bear arms

Everyone living in the United States is entitled to the above rights which are outlined in the Bill of Rights.

66. What do we show loyalty to when we say the Pledge of Allegiance?*

- The United States
- The flag

The Pledge of Allegiance is an oath that expresses allegiance to the flag and to the country.

"I pledge allegiance to the flag of the United States of America, and to the Republic for which it stands, one nation under God, indivisible, with liberty and justice for all."

67. Name two promises that new citizens make in the Oath of Allegiance.

- Give up loyalty to other countries
- Defend the (U.S.) Constitution
- Obey the laws of the United States
- Serve in the military (if needed)
- Serve (help, do important work for) the nation (if needed)
- Be loyal to the United States

The Oath of Allegiance asks citizens to promise to defend the U.S., give up loyalty to other countries, serve in the military or elsewhere if needed, and to obey U.S. laws.

"I hereby declare, on oath, that I absolutely and entirely renounce and abjure all allegiance and fidelity to any foreign prince, potentate, state, or sovereignty of whom or which I have heretofore been a subject or citizen; that I will support and defend the Constitution and laws of the United States of America against all enemies, foreign and domestic; that I will bear true faith and allegiance to the same; that I will bear arms on behalf of the United States when required by the law; that I will perform noncombatant service in the Armed Forces of the United States when required by the law; that I will perform work of national importance under civilian direction when required by the law; and that I take this obligation freely without any mental reservation or purpose of evasion; so help me God."

68. How can people become United States citizens?

- Be born in the United States, under the conditions set by the 14th Amendment
- Naturalize
- Derive citizenship (under conditions set by Congress)

The path to citizenship in the United States can be as simple as being born in the U.S. under specific conditions. Otherwise, it may necessitate naturalization by meeting certain requirements, or it may be derived in some circumstances from a parent being naturalized.

69. What are <u>two</u> examples of civic participation in the United States?

- Vote
- Run for office
- Join a political party
- Help with a campaign
- Join a civic group
- Join a community group
- Give an elected official your opinion (on an issue)
- Contact elected officials
- Support or oppose an issue or policy
- Write to a newspaper

Since the U.S. government is a representative democracy, it is important for citizens to participate in the democratic process. This is so they can have representation. Citizens elect officials. These officials represent citizens' concerns for the country. Part of participating in the democratic process is voting, calling senators and representatives, expressing public opinions, and helping with campaigns.

70. What is <u>one</u> way Americans can serve their country?

- Vote
- Pay taxes
- Obey the law
- Serve in the military
- Run for office
- Work for local, state, or federal government

There are many ways for Americans to serve their country. Some, such as paying taxes and obeying the law, are required. Others, such as voting, serving in the military, and running for office, are generally optional.

71. Why is it important to pay federal taxes?

- Required by law
- All people pay to fund the federal government
- Required by the (U.S.) Constitution (16th Amendment)
- Civic duty

Federal taxes enable the federal government to provide services and fund programs as allocated by Congress. National income tax was ratified as law by the 16th Amendment in 1913, and paying these taxes is a core civic duty.

72. It is important for all men age 18 through 25 to register for the Selective Service. Name <u>one</u> reason why.

- Required by law
- Civic duty
- Makes the draft fair, if needed

The Selected Service is a United States agency that keeps information on those who may be up for a draft. All male U.S. citizens and male immigrant non-citizens must register within 30 days of their 18th birthdays.

American History

Colonial Period and Independence

73. The colonists came to America for many reasons. Name <u>one</u>.

- Freedom
- Political liberty
- Religious freedom
- Economic opportunity
- Escape persecution

European colonists came to America from England, France, Spain, and the Netherlands in the late 16th century. They wanted to escape persecution. They also wanted political and religious freedom.

74. Who lived in America before the Europeans arrived?*

- American Indians
- Native Americans

American Indians are indigenous to the United States. Today there are 562 Native American tribes in the United States. The Cherokee, Sioux, and Navajo are the largest tribes.

75. What group of people was taken and sold as slaves?

- Africans
- People from Africa

Slavery in America began in 1619. It ended in 1865 after the Civil War and with the adoption of the 13th Amendment.

76. What war did the Americans fight to win independence from Britain?

- American Revolution
- The (American) Revolutionary War
- War for (American) Independence

The American Revolution, which broadly lasted from 1765-1783, was a conflict that allowed the thirteen American colonies to gain independence from Great Britain and secure a free United States of America.

77. Name one reason why the Americans declared independence from Britain.

- High taxes
- Taxation without representation
- British soldiers stayed in Americans' houses (boarding, quartering)
- They did not have self-government
- Boston Massacre
- Boston Tea Party (Tea Act)
- Stamp Act
- Sugar Act
- Townshend Acts
- Intolerable (Coercive) Acts

The colonists fought the British because they wanted independence from Britain. The colonists felt that King George III and the British army were taking advantage through high taxes and boarding laws. The colonists were not self-governed but wanted freedom from tyranny.

78. Who wrote the Declaration of Independence?*

- (Thomas) Jefferson

The Declaration of Independence was written by Thomas Jefferson in June 1776.

79. When was the Declaration of Independence adopted?

- July 4, 1776

Congress ratified the Declaration of Independence on July 4, 1776. The Declaration of Independence explains that the Thirteen Colonies were independent from the rule of Britain.

80. The American Revolution had many important events. Name <u>one</u>.

- (Battle of) Bunker Hill
- Declaration of Independence
- Washington Crossing the Delaware (Battle of Trenton)
- (Battle of) Saratoga
- Valley Forge (Encampment)
- (Battle of) Yorktown (British surrender at Yorktown)

There was not one single event that determined the outcome of the American Revolution. It was comprised of a series of battles and maneuvers over several years, along with political events like the signing of the Declaration of Independence.

81. There were 13 original states. Name five.

- New Hampshire
- Massachusetts
- Rhode Island
- Connecticut
- New York
- New Jersey
- Pennsylvania
- Delaware
- Maryland
- Virginia
- North Carolina
- South Carolina
- Georgia

The thirteen colonies were originally British colonies on the North American Atlantic coast. They were founded in the 17th and 18th centuries.

82. What founding document was written in 1787?

- (U.S.) Constitution

The Constitution was written in 1787 during the Constitutional Convention.

83. The Federalist Papers supported the passage of the U.S. Constitution. Name <u>one</u> of the writers.

- (James) Madison
- (Alexander) Hamilton
- (John) Jay
- Publius

The Federalist Papers were written to advocate for the ratification of the Constitution. James Madison, Alexander Hamilton, and John Jay wrote under the pseudonym "Publius."

84. Why were the Federalist Papers important?

- They helped people understand the (U.S.) Constitution.
- They supported passing the (U.S.) Constitution.

The Federalist Papers were essays written to help Americans better understand the U.S. Constitution, the reasoning behind it, and its goals. It was designed to sway voters toward ratification of the Constitution.

85. Benjamin Franklin is famous for many things. Name <u>one</u>.

- Founded the first free public libraries
- First Postmaster General of the United States
- Helped write the Declaration of Independence
- Inventor
- U.S. diplomat

Benjamin Franklin was a diplomat, statesman, inventor, humorist, civic activist, scientist, politician, political theorist, author, printer, freemason, and postmaster. He is well-known for his discoveries relating to electricity. He also founded civic organizations. Franklin was a delegate at the Constitutional Convention. He signed all four major documents relating to the founding of the United States.

86. George Washington is famous for many things. Name <u>one</u>.*

- "Father of Our Country"
- First president of the United States
- General of the Continental Army
- President of the Constitutional Convention

The first president of the United States, George Washington (1732–1799) was also the General of the Continental Army during the American Revolution.

Washington set several precedents for the office of the President.

87. Thomas Jefferson is famous for many things. Name <u>one</u>.

- Writer of the Declaration of Independence
- Third president of the United States
- Doubled the size of the United States (Louisiana Purchase)
- First Secretary of State
- Founded the University of Virginia
- Writer of the Virginia Statute on Religious Freedom

Before becoming the third president of the United States, Thomas Jefferson (1743–1826) was the primary writer of the Declaration of Independence, and the nation's first Secretary of State. During his presidency, he enacted the Louisiana Purchase by buying land from France which doubled the size of the United States.

88. James Madison is famous for many things. Name <u>one</u>.

- "Father of the Constitution"
- Fourth president of the United States
- President during the War of 1812
- One of the writers of the Federalist Papers

James Madison (1751–1836), the United States' fourth president, was known as the "Father of the Constitution" for his role in creating the Constitution and for gaining popular support for the document, partly as one of the writers of the Federalist Papers.

89. Alexander Hamilton is famous for many things. Name <u>one</u>.

- First Secretary of the Treasury
- One of the writers of the Federalist Papers
- Helped establish the First Bank of the United States
- Aide to General George Washington
- Member of the Continental Congress

Alexander Hamilton was the primary writer of most of the Federalist Papers, and his views on government helped shape the government of the fledgling United States of America and its financial system.

1800s

90. What territory did the United States buy from France in 1803?

- Louisiana Territory
- Louisiana

The buying of this land is known as the Louisiana Purchase. It allowed the U.S. to gain 827,000 square miles of land for $15 million.

91. Name <u>one</u> war fought by the United States in the 1800s.

- War of 1812
- Mexican-American War
- Civil War
- Spanish-American War

A total of four wars were fought by the U.S. in the 1800s. The War of 1812 was between the U.S. and Great Britain. The Mexican-American War was between the U.S. and Mexico. The Civil War was between the American North and South. The Spanish-American War was between the U.S. and Spain.

92. Name the U.S. war between the North and the South.

- The Civil War

The Civil War was fought from 1861 to 1865 with around 620,000 deaths. The South seceded as the Confederate States of America with Jefferson Davis as the President. Abraham Lincoln was President of the Union.

93. The Civil War had many important events. Name one.

- (Battle of) Fort Sumter
- Emancipation Proclamation
- (Battle of) Vicksburg
- (Battle of) Gettysburg
- Sherman's March
- (Surrender at) Appomattox
- (Battle of) Antietam/Sharpsburg
- Lincoln was assassinated.

The brief attack on Fort Sumter was the opening battle of the Civil War. Fighting between the United States and the Confederate States would continue in battles and skirmishes for several years across much of the country. After the war, President Abraham Lincoln was assassinated by John Wilkes Booth.

94. Abraham Lincoln is famous for many things. Name <u>one</u>.*

- Freed the slaves (Emancipation Proclamation)
- Saved (or preserved) the Union
- Led the United States during the Civil War
- 16th president of the United States
- Delivered the Gettysburg Address

Abraham Lincoln issued the Emancipation Proclamation on January 1, 1863. This document freed all slaves in the Confederacy. Lincoln was also the Commander-in-Chief during the Civil War. He effectively saved the Union during a time of war.

95. What did the Emancipation Proclamation do?

- Freed the slaves
- Freed slaves in the Confederacy
- Freed slaves in the Confederate states
- Freed slaves in most Southern states

The Emancipation Proclamation was issued in the third year of the Civil War. This document granted slaves freedom within the rebel states.

96. What U.S. war ended slavery?

- The Civil War

The American North and South disagreed over the economics of slavery. They also disagreed on expanding the institution of slavery into new territories in the West. These disagreements brought up the question of states' rights under a central government.

97. What amendment says all persons born or naturalized in the United States, and subject to the jurisdiction thereof, are U.S. citizens?

- 14th Amendment

Ratified in 1868, the 14th Amendment's Section 1 describes citizenship for all persons born or naturalized in the United States, and goes on to state that no law will limit the privileges or immunities of citizens, nor "deprive any person of life, liberty, or property, without due process of law."

98. When did all men get the right to vote?

- After the Civil War
- During Reconstruction
- (With the) 15th Amendment
- 1870

The 15th Amendment, while brief, clearly states that "the right of citizens of the United States to vote shall not be denied or abridged ... on account of race, color, or previous condition of servitude," granting all male citizens the right to vote.

99. Name **one** leader of the women's rights movement in the 1800s.

- Susan B. Anthony
- Elizabeth Cady Stanton
- Sojourner Truth
- Harriet Tubman
- Lucretia Mott
- Lucy Stone

While women did not gain the right to vote in the United States until 1920, many women in the 1800s worked to ensure rights for women in other areas, such as in education, in their professional lives, and in the ownership of property.

Recent American History and Other Important Historical Information

100. Name one war fought by the United States in the 1900s.

- World War I
- World War II
- Korean War
- Vietnam War
- (Persian) Gulf War

Five wars were fought by the U.S. in the 1900s. The U.S. joined the Allied Powers during World War I in 1917 against Germany, Austria-Hungary, Bulgaria, and the Ottoman Empire (the Central Powers). The United States joined the Allies during World War II in 1941 and fought Japan, Germany, and Italy (the Axis). The U.S. allied with South Korea in the Korean War from 1950 to 1953, and again they fought with South Vietnam against North Vietnam from 1959 to 1973. The Persian Gulf War lasted from 1990 to 1991 against Iraq as a response to Iraq's invasion of Kuwait.

101. Why did the United States enter World War I?

- Because Germany attacked U.S. (civilian) ships
- To support the Allied Powers (England, France, Italy, and Russia)
- To oppose the Central Powers (Germany, Austria-Hungary, the Ottoman Empire, and Bulgaria)

After almost three years of neutrality in the Great War, President Woodrow Wilson asked Congress to declare war on Germany in April of 1917. German attacks on U.S. and other nations' civilian ships such as the RMS Lusitania changed Americans' views on the war, and Germany's blunders in diplomacy such as the Zimmermann telegram also turned American sentiment toward entering the war. Joining the conflict was also meant to support America's strongest economic and political partners, such as England and France.

102. When did all women get the right to vote?

- 1920
- After World War I
- (With the) 19th Amendment

1920's 19th Amendment states that "the right of citizens of the United States to vote shall not be denied or abridged ... on account of sex."

103. What was the Great Depression?

- Longest economic recession in modern history

After the stock market crash of 1929, the Great Depression was more than a decade of financial crisis and economic recession in the United States. Production and employment dropped quickly, and a series of banking panics and international financial issues prolonged the effects. It wasn't until heavy military spending began for World War II that America began to pull out of the Great Depression.

104. When did the Great Depression start?

- The Great Crash (1929)
- Stock market crash of 1929

The Great Depression began on October 28, 1929, when the stock market crashed nearly 25 percent over the course of just two days.

105. Who was president during the Great Depression and World War II?

- (Franklin) Roosevelt

Franklin Roosevelt (1882-1945), also known as FDR, became president in 1933, four years after the start of the Great Depression. Roosevelt expanded government programs and launched many reforms designed to blunt the negative impact of the Great Depression and start the country on the path to recovery. Additionally, he was the president during most of World War II, staying in office until his death in 1945, less than a year before the official end of the conflict.

106. Why did the United States enter World War II?

- (Bombing of) Pearl Harbor
- Japanese attacked Pearl Harbor
- To support the Allied Powers (England, France, and Russia)
- To oppose the Axis Powers (Germany, Italy, and Japan)

The bombing of Pearl Harbor on December 7, 1941 while the United States was still officially neutral in the war was seen as an act in need of retaliation, and proved to be the last provocation before the U.S. began active combat against the Axis Powers. The United States declared war on Japan the next day, December 8, and declared war on Germany and Italy a few days later.

107. Dwight Eisenhower is famous for many things. Name <u>one</u>.

- General during World War II
- President at the end of (during) the Korean War
- 34th president of the United States
- Signed the Federal-Aid Highway Act of 1956 (Created the Interstate System)

Dwight Eisenhower (1890-1969) was the Supreme Commander of the Allied Expeditionary Force in Europe during World War II, which included planning the essential Normandy landings in June 1944. He was also the United States' 34th president, and led Congress to adopt the Federal Aid Highway Act of 1956 to build infrastructure for economic and military reasons.

108. Who was the United States' main rival during the Cold War?

- Soviet Union
- USSR
- Russia

The Union of Soviet Socialist Republics (USSR) was a federal union comprised of many national republics in eastern Europe and Asia. Its communist government was highly centralized in Russia and its capital, Moscow.

109. During the Cold War, what was <u>one</u> main concern of the United States?

- Communism
- Nuclear war

The Cold War was a state of rivalry between the Soviet Union and the United States after World War II. The Cold War lasted for about 45 years as the United States promised to stop communism while the Soviet Union worked to expand it. While here was officially no direct fighting between the United States and the Soviet Union, both sides amassed large arsenals of nuclear weapons and prepared for a cataclysmic nuclear war which ultimately never occurred.

110. Why did the United States enter the Korean War?

- To stop the spread of communism

In the Korean War (1950-1953), North Korea was a communist state supported by China and the Soviet Union, while South Korea was supported by the United States and its anti-communist allies. The allies feared that if South Korea fell to communism, other nearby countries would also be vulnerable to communist takeover.

111. Why did the United States enter the Vietnam War?

- To stop the spread of communism

Like with other conflicts in the region, the United States believed that if Vietnam became a communist country, it would cause other nations in the region to lean toward communism. This is a part of what is known as the Domino Theory. After the U.S. withdrawal from Vietnam in 1973, Vietnam and the neighboring countries of Laos and Cambodia did eventually become communist states.

112. What did the civil rights movement do?

- Fought to end racial discrimination

The Civil Rights Movement took place during the 1950s and 1960s. It was a social justice movement for African Americans and other minorities to gain equal rights in the United States.

113. Martin Luther King, Jr. is famous for many things. Name one.*

- Fought for civil rights
- Worked for equality for all Americans
- Worked to ensure that people would "not be judged by the color of their skin, but by the content of their character"

Martin Luther King Jr. was a Baptist minister and activist. He was the primary spokesperson during the Civil Rights movement. King led nonviolent protests, organized marches, and encouraged civil disobedience. King was assassinated in 1968 in Tennessee.

114. Why did the United States enter the Persian Gulf War?

- To force the Iraqi military from Kuwait

The Persian Gulf War in 1990 and 1991, was the result of Iraq, led by Saddam Hussein, invading and occupying the neighboring country of Kuwait. In response, the United States and 41 allied countries entered the conflict to free Kuwait from the occupation and drive the Iraqi attackers out.

115. What major event happened on September 11, 2001 in the United States?*

- Terrorists attacked the United States
- Terrorists took over two planes and crashed them into the World Trade Center in New York City
- Terrorists took over a plane and crashed into the Pentagon in Arlington, Virginia
- Terrorists took over a plane originally aimed at Washington, D.C., and crashed in a field in Pennsylvania

The attacks of 9/11 happened when the Islamic terrorist group, al-Qaeda, hijacked four passenger airliners. The terrorists crashed them into the World Trade Center's North and South towers, the Pentagon, and a field in Pennsylvania.

116. Name <u>one</u> U.S. military conflict after the September 11, 2001 attacks.

- (Global) War on Terror
- War in Afghanistan
- War in Iraq

The U.S. military has been deployed to many countries since 2001, mainly in the Middle East. In addition to the wars in Afghanistan and Iraq, the War on Terror saw American military conflicts in Syria, Libya, Yemen, Somalia, and other areas.

117. Name <u>one</u> American Indian tribe in the United States.

- Apache
- Blackfeet
- Cayuga
- Cherokee
- Cheyenne
- Chippewa
- Choctaw
- Creek
- Crow
- Hopi
- Huron
- Inupiat
- Lakota
- Mohawk
- Mohegan
- Navajo
- Oneida
- Onondaga
- Pueblo
- Seminole
- Seneca
- Shawnee
- Sioux
- Teton
- Tuscarora

118. Name <u>one</u> example of an American innovation.

- Light bulb
- Automobile (cars, internal combustion engine)
- Skyscrapers
- Airplane
- Assembly line
- Landing on the moon
- Integrated circuit (IC)

The United States of America has a proud history of technological innovation. Development of the light bulb brightened American cities that grew ever taller with the age of skyscrapers. After the Wright Brothers flew a heavier-than-air powered airplane in 1903, American innovations led to the application of technology to land on the moon in 1969.

Symbols and Holidays

Symbols

119. What is the capital of the United States?

- Washington, D.C.

Washington D.C. became the capital of the United States in 1790 when the Residence Act was signed. The District of Columbia is not part of any state. It was made to serve as a federal district under the authority of Congress.

120. Where is the Statue of Liberty?

- New York (Harbor)
- Liberty Island [Also acceptable are New Jersey, near New York City, and on the Hudson (River).]

The Statue of Liberty was a gift to the United States from France. It is meant to honor the friendship between the two countries. The statue is a robed Roman liberty goddess named Libertas. She holds a message on her tablet that says July 4, 1776 (Independence Day) in roman numerals.

121. Why does the flag have 13 stripes?*

- (Because there were) 13 original colonies
- (Because the stripes) represent the original colonies

The flag has 13 stripes. They symbolize the 13 colonies that declared their independence from Great Britain.

122. Why does the flag have 50 stars?

- (Because there is) one star for each state
- (Because) each star represents a state
- (Because there are) 50 states

The stars on the American flag stand for the 50 states. A star was added each time the U.S. took on a state. Hawaii was the last state added in 1959.

123. What is the name of the national anthem?

- The Star-Spangled Banner

Francis Scott Key wrote the Star-Spangled Banner in 1814. He wrote it after the Battle of Baltimore during the War of 1812.

"O say can you see, by the dawn's early light,
What so proudly we hailed at the twilight's last gleaming,

Whose broad stripes and bright stars through the perilous fight,
O'er the ramparts we watched were so gallantly streaming?
And the rocket's red glare, the bombs bursting in air,
Gave proof through the night that our flag was still there.
O say does that star-spangled banner yet wave
O'er the land of the free and the home of the brave?"

124. The Nation's first motto was "E Pluribus Unum." What does that mean?

- Out of many, one
- We all become one

The Latin phrase "E Pluribus Unum" was chosen in 1782 as a motto to represent that in the formation of the United States out of the Thirteen Colonies, many became one.

Holidays

125. What is Independence Day?

- A holiday to celebrate U.S. independence (from Britain)
- The country's birthday

July 4 is the day the Declaration of Independence was published in 1776.

126. Name <u>three</u> national U.S. holidays.*

- New Year's Day
- Martin Luther King, Jr. Day
- Presidents Day (Washington's Birthday)
- Memorial Day
- Independence Day
- Labor Day
- Columbus Day
- Veterans Day
- Thanksgiving Day
- Christmas Day

National holidays are recognized by the U.S. government. Federal employees are paid on national holidays. Also, non-essential federal government offices are closed.

127. What is Memorial Day?

- A holiday to honor soldiers who died in military service

Memorial Day was first observed in 1868 to honor those that had died in the Civil War. Now celebrated on the last Monday of May each year, it continues to remember and honor all American soldiers who died in service to their country.

128. What is Veterans Day?

- A holiday to honor people in the (U.S.) military
- A holiday to honor people who have served (in the U.S. military)

Veterans Day honors current and former members of the United States Armed Forces, and has been officially celebrated as such since 1954. Veterans Day is observed each November 11.

Test Yourself

1. What is the form of government of the United States?

2. What is the supreme law of the land? *

3. Name one thing the U.S. Constitution does.

4. The U.S. Constitution starts with the words "We the People." What does "We the People" mean?

5. How are changes made to the U.S. Constitution?

6. What does the Bill of Rights protect?

7. How many amendments does the U.S. Constitution have? *

8. Why is the Declaration of Independence important?

9. What founding document said the American colonies were free from Britain?

10. Name two important ideas from the Declaration of Independence and the U.S. Constitution.

11. The words "Life, Liberty, and the pursuit of Happiness" are in what founding document?

12. What is the economic system of the United States? *

13. What is the rule of law?

14. Many documents influenced the U.S. Constitution. Name one.

15. There are three branches of government. Why?

16. Name the three branches of government.

17. The President of the United States is in charge of which branch of government?

18. What part of the federal government writes laws?

19. What are the two parts of the U.S. Congress?

20. Name one power of the U.S. Congress. *

21. How many U.S. senators are there?

22. How long is a term for a U.S. senator?

23. Who is one of your state's U.S. senators now?

24. How many voting members are in the House of Representatives?

25. How long is a term for a member of the House of Representatives?

26. Why do U.S. representatives serve shorter terms than U.S. senators?

27. How many senators does each state have?

28. Why does each state have two senators?

29. Name your U.S. representative.

30. What is the name of the Speaker of the House of Representatives now? *

31. Who does a U.S. senator represent?

32. Who elects U.S. senators?

33. Who does a member of the House of Representatives represent?

34. Who elects members of the House of Representatives?

35. Some states have more representatives than other states. Why?

36. The President of the United States is elected for how many years? *

37. The President of the United States can serve only two terms. Why?

38. What is the name of the President of the United States now? *

39. What is the name of the Vice President of the United States now? *

40. If the president can no longer serve, who becomes president?

41. Name one power of the president.

42. Who is Commander in Chief of the U.S. military?

43. Who signs bills to become laws?

44. Who vetoes bills? *

45. Who appoints federal judges?

46. The executive branch has many parts. Name one.

47. What does the President's Cabinet do?

48. What are two Cabinet-level positions?

49. Why is the Electoral College important?

50. What is one part of the judicial branch?

51. What does the judicial branch do?

52. What is the highest court in the United States? *

53. How many seats are on the Supreme Court?

54. How many Supreme Court justices are usually needed to decide a case?

55. How long do Supreme Court justices serve?

56. Supreme Court justices serve for life. Why?

57. Who is the Chief Justice of the United States now?

58. Name one power that is only for the federal government.

59. Name one power that is only for the states.

60. What is the purpose of the 10th Amendment?

61. Who is the governor of your state now? *

62. What is the capital of your state?

63. There are four amendments to the U.S. Constitution about who can vote. Describe one of them.

64. Who can vote in federal elections, run for federal office, and serve on a jury in the United States?

65. What are three rights of everyone living in the United States?

66. What do we show loyalty to when we say the Pledge of Allegiance? *

67. Name two promises that new citizens make in the Oath of Allegiance.

68. How can people become United States citizens?

69. What are two examples of civic participation in the United States?

70. What is one-way Americans can serve their country?

71. Why is it important to pay federal taxes?

72. It is important for all men age 18 through 25 to register for the Selective Service. Name one reason why.

73. The colonists came to America for many reasons. Name one.

74. Who lived in America before the Europeans arrived? *

75. What group of people was taken and sold as slaves?

76. What war did the Americans fight to win independence from Britain?

77. Name one reason why the Americans declared independence from Britain.

78. Who wrote the Declaration of Independence? *

79. When was the Declaration of Independence adopted?

80. The American Revolution had many important events. Name one.

81. There were 13 original states. Name five.

82. What founding document was written in 1787?

83. The Federalist Papers supported the passage of the U.S. Constitution. Name one of the writers.

84. Why were the Federalist Papers important?

85. Benjamin Franklin is famous for many things. Name one.

86. George Washington is famous for many things. Name one. *

87. Thomas Jefferson is famous for many things. Name one.

88. James Madison is famous for many things. Name one.

89. Alexander Hamilton is famous for many things. Name one.

90. What territory did the United States buy from France in 1803?

91. Name one war fought by the United States in the 1800s.

92. Name the U.S. war between the North and the South.

93. The Civil War had many important events. Name one.

94. Abraham Lincoln is famous for many things. Name one. *

95. What did the Emancipation Proclamation do?

96. What U.S. war ended slavery?

97. What amendment says all persons born or naturalized in the United States, and subject to the jurisdiction thereof, are U.S. citizens?

98. When did all men get the right to vote?

99. Name one leader of the women's rights movement in the 1800s.

100. Name one war fought by the United States in the 1900s.

101. Why did the United States enter World War I?

102. When did all women get the right to vote?

103. What was the Great Depression?

104. When did the Great Depression start?

105. Who was president during the Great Depression and World War II?

106. Why did the United States enter World War II?

107. Dwight Eisenhower is famous for many things. Name one.

108. Who was the United States' main rival during the Cold War?

109. During the Cold War, what was one main concern of the United States?

110. Why did the United States enter the Korean War?

111. Why did the United States enter the Vietnam War?

112. What did the civil rights movement do?

113. Martin Luther King, Jr. is famous for many things. Name one. *

114. Why did the United States enter the Persian Gulf War?

115. What major event happened on September 11, 2001 in the United States? *

116. Name one U.S. military conflict after the September 11, 2001 attacks.

117. Name one American Indian tribe in the United States.

118. Name one example of an American innovation.

119. What is the capital of the United States?

120. Where is the Statue of Liberty?

121. Why does the flag have 13 stripes? *

122. Why does the flag have 50 stars?

123. What is the name of the national anthem?

124. The Nation's first motto was "E Pluribus Unum." What does that mean?

125. What is Independence Day?

126. Name three national U.S. holidays. *

127. What is Memorial Day?

128. What is Veterans Day?

www.ingramcontent.com/pod-product-compliance
Lightning Source LLC
Chambersburg PA
CBHW050656160426
43194CB00010B/1966